The
Empirical Observations
of Algernon

The
Empirical Observations
of Algernon

Iain Cameron Williams

i will publishing
ISBN 9781916146501
revised edition

cover design: Cath Medrano
photography: Iain Cameron Williams

Author's Note

This book is a series of impressions collected on my travels during 2018 from February through to May, which included a visit to the USA and Canada. There is little need by way of this note for me to list my itinerary as my journey becomes self-explanatory through my accounts.

Some of the narratives give an insight into how an Englishman abroad observes his foreign surroundings. Some observations are purely doodles related as and when I encounter them.

Some text is witty, some light-hearted. Most of it is written in the present. When I encounter a situation or location that interests me, I allow my surroundings to speak. From this standpoint, I am an observer and a listener, and as such, I create a picture with words. I try to record the accounts instantaneously, although I've had to rely on the image in my memory on some occasions.

My original concept was to write a diary to amuse myself while taking my evening meals. Hence, several of these observations are written in restaurants. From that seed, I expanded my idea. *The Empirical Observations of Algernon* is that vision.[1]

I. C. Williams
June 2019

---

[1] Algernon was the nickname given to me by my father when I was a young teenager. I later discovered the name derives from the 1966 novel *Flowers for Algernon* by Daniel Keyes.

Contents

America (II) - March 2018

England - April/May 2018

take a leaf ...

take a leaf ...

take a leaf ... any leaf
hold it close to your heart
tell a story to a stranger
only then will you reveal
exactly who you are

take a leaf ... any leaf
throw it to the stars
watch it fall a thousand pieces
the innocence of anger
patterns who we are

take a leaf ... any leaf
fold it neatly into corners
label it with love
seldom do we listen
to the sweeping of a brush

take a leaf ... any leaf
now the tree is bare
the forest is no longer
he that holds the candle bright
will light the path ahead

England

Sunshine on my Shoes

The shake of an umbrella.
A purposeful step.
Shivering, huddled together, sheltering beneath canopies.
Darting stragglers with no destination in sight.
Where are the seagulls?
No one thinks to ask.
A swift Scotch in the bar in the hope that the rain will soon pass.
The evening newspaper that won't smell of vinegar and chips
cast upon the sidewalk without a say.
Print dribbling into the drain.
A mercenary look from an uncomplicated cat
drenched in mink,
sidling beneath a barrel of garbage.
No one thought to ask.
There's no sunshine on my shoes,
and the lights in John Lewis have now been turned off.
It must be all of eight o'clock.
It's raining still.
The disappointing sound of rain …

It's raining still.

Jamie's Italian, Liverpool (dinner)
February 8

Choose a Doorway

Choose a doorway,
any doorway,
make yourself at home.
Pick a number,
any number
in the keyhole lottery.
Carrier bags
and a rolled-up duvet
make for the common touch.
A hot bevy or two,
a can of Special Brew
to keep the cold wind at bay.
Sleep in a doorway.
Any doorway will do.

Liverpool
February 8

The Three Graces, Liverpool

The Geography of the Ocean [2]

The constant sea,
like an unloved melody.
Obtrusive, unnerving, belching.
Spewing forth its guts upon a shameless shoreline.
Ripping out the cartilage of its very existence.
A futile action
as old as man.
But still without a constant friend.
The lonely sea.
Alone.
Fiercely fighting its corner of the planet.

Jury's Waterfront, Brighton (breakfast)
February 13

---

[2] This account was written during breakfast at Jury's Waterfront, Brighton, as I gazed out at the tempestuous sea and stormy weather, and is inspired by and dedicated to my great-grandfather John Francon Williams who in 1881 had his monumental geographical work *The Geography of the Oceans* published.

Botticelli or Not

Angels come in all shapes and sizes. The larger, more voluptuous variety find it more challenging to sit atop church domes and such, whereas the slimmer, svelte species think nothing of dangling from ornamental pediments if only to add a little decorative touch. Fashion, not being the dictator here: done more in a watchful, protective stance. Some are angels of mercy; some are of mirth. Some are too darn lazy to get off their backsides. Others take flight like wind in a kite. Lest we forget, what Putti, Eros, and Aphrodite all have in common are wings. Such things are not to be sniffed at. Attached on the back, they flip, and they flap, and then flap and flip on their way back. We all have an angel, whether we befriend it or not. It's solely up to you if it's a Rubens, Botticelli, or Baroque.

Brighton
February 13

Rubens, Botticelli, or Baroque

I Will

Rain sodden.
Trodden in
puddles as deep as a deep-pan pizza.
It's Valentine's Night.
What a fright.
Halloween, more like.

I'm fortunate to get a table.
The *maître d'* told me
he'd already turned one couple away.
I overheard one waiter reveal
he'd been toiling since nine in the morning.
It was now 9:30 p.m.

They're low on spinach,
apparently so.
Something to do with the ratio.

At the end of my meal,
when I came to pay,
my voucher was declined.
Instead,
I was offered
a reduction
off my bill,
to which I replied, 'I will.'

Zizzi, Brighton (dinner)
February 14

Old Souls

Photographs of old Brighton chatter.
They decorate the walls
telling me their story.
Every person inside the frame is dead.
That said,
it breaks my heart,
not in a way Adele might sing,
more in a factual, historical sense.
The thought that every single person
in each picture
had as much life as you or me
haunts me.
Now they are gone
to places higher.
Places we can only dream of
in the hope
we might one day belong.
Old souls live on.

Just before I departed
the waitress gave me a couple of imperial mints.
Old souls live on.

Bankers, Brighton (dinner)
February 15

Ready to Eat

Ready to eat.
I sat downstairs.
It was less busy.
Room to sit comfortably and digest the day's happenings.
Halfway through my meal,
I watched four refuse collectors
dressed in brilliant fluorescent yellow jackets
carry out the rubbish
straight through the restaurant.
Yes, four refuse collectors
carrying polythene bags filled with garbage.
Waste up to their waist.
Cardboard and plastic, heading for the sea.
How did we get to this point in civilization?
John was so correct with his warning in *the Geography of the Oceans*.
Like ready to wear,
plastic never forgets.

Pret a Manger (dinner)
13 Hanover Square, Mayfair, London
February 16

Burlington Arcade, Mayfair, London

Victoria Memorial, London

What I See

What I see is not necessarily there;
a NASA spacesuit,
the clutter of cutlery being placed upon tabletops,
"Hello."
"Hello," came back the reply.
A cake delivery.
The sun shining across the sea
motionless, like me.
Waiting for a cue.
Screaming children invade the lobby.
A temporary hobby
dismissed at the sight of free orange juice.
Behind every great fortune is at least one crime.
There's nothing new in anything anymore;
we've heard it all a million times or more,
multiplied by four.
I still find it difficult believing Bowie's dead.
Addie always said she wasn't going anywhere, [3]
that she would always be here.
She remained true to her word.
I wonder if Bowie will do the same.

Hilton Metropole, Brighton (breakfast)
February 17

---

[3] Addie refers to the jazz singer Adelaide Hall.

12

Brighton Museum and Art Gallery

"She's quite pregnant with twins," relayed the honey-haired lady into her mobile. The news reverberated along the museum corridor. As she spoke, it was as if she was floating on a gust of wind.
I smiled, an impassive glance, which she acknowledged with a bow of her head.
Slowly I moved away between the oil paintings, collecting my thoughts. The images appeared static upon a storm of muted color.
My uncle Sydney passed away yesterday evening. The news arrived via a text message and, for a minute or two, made me stop what I was doing. My mother's brother: the last of the Rex/Smith siblings to close the door. What saddens me is that I never knew him, especially as he was my mother's youngest brother and probably her fondest.
In the gift shop in the museum lobby, a Biba book attracted my attention and hauled me back to High Street Kensington in the 1970s. How can I not sense a longing for that era? The photographs bring back so many memories, moments so close I feel I can almost touch them. I recoil. A sense of déjà vu withers into the here and now. I reassure myself the Biba store is sorely missed. A book of recollections just doesn't amount to anything. I place the book back on the shelf and head out into the afternoon.

Brighton Museum and Art Gallery, Brighton
February 21

Hotel Buena Vista

Two lean waiters,
thin as a crisp,
stand at their station,
dishing the dish.
Polishing cutlery,
wiping a brow.
Pristine starched aprons
tied at the bow.
Time is a madam
that orders off-piste.
Custom has fallen
at the Hotel Buena Vista.
Now the two waiters
fold napkins all day
with no one to wait on
and nothing to say.

London
February 25

Pastrami on Rye

Look me in the eye.
Are you truly Mr. Lawrence?
I showed you a likeness
that mirrored your surprise.
Amy's on the soundtrack
plying me with good vibes.
Tori's in a telephone box.
She'll soon be on your dial.

The street is real empty,
and it's only six twenty-five.
I wonder where to eat.
Seagulls walking on the beach.
New York's on the horizon,
pastrami on rye.
Bet your bottom dollar
D.H. Lawrence never died.

St Paul's Cafe, Worthing, and Worthing seafront
March 5

six o'clock on Worthing Pier

Heaven on a Platter (shack alack, shack alack)

It's a serious business
this eating of fish.
A loss of concentration
and a bone might spike your gum.
God forbid I should swallow one.
Fresh local bream
steamed in lemon fish stock
with whole green olives and cherry tomatoes.
Take your time,
savor every bite.
Allow the flesh to kiss your palette,
and you'll be fine.
At the Crabshack
  shack alack, shack alack
Where the disco music licks your ears
Heaven on a platter
At the Crabshack
  shack alack, shack alack
It truly is
Heaven on a platter
At the Crabshack
  shack alack, shack alack

Crabshack, Worthing (dinner)
March 7

Main: 'Catch of the Day'
Pan roasted local whole sea bream with new potatoes, tomatoes, green olives,
basil, lemon, white wine, and olive oil £17
Pudding: Homemade warm orange, honey, almond and polenta cake with
whipped cream £6

at the Crabshack, shack alack, shack alack

'My friends look like crabs,' cried out a French lady
to her husband sitting at the table next to me.

America (I)

The Roger Hotel

So the Roger
has a lodger,
and that lodger is me.
Ensconced in a suite
that suits
my personality.
With a bed
the size of a monster crab,
and a crib
for a bath
more cramped
than a lavatory,
and a TV screen
as big as a wall
that makes me
look so small.

The Roger New York, NYC
March 14

New York (I)

New York's destruction
is rampant
and ongoing.
The city
is a mess,
with construction sites
taking over
practically every other street corner.
Sidewalks are bleeding,
crying out to be cleansed
of smelly feet.
The Council
unheeding.
A catastrophe
of sorts
is taking place
right before Liberty's eyes.
Are you really oblivious to it?

The white man walks
when the red hand decrees.
There's little that I can do
to alter the traffic flow.
Manhattan has changed
since the eighteen years
I was last here.
It's a sign of the times,
and not for the better.
The Avenues are wounded.
Sad reminders of times lost.

Mindless destruction.
Whole blocks are missing.
Wanton greed.
Whoever heard
of Madison
and Thirty-third.
A square garden
is what I need.

Walk.
Don't walk.
Lift up your feet.
Spare me a dime, brother.
I'm down on my knees,
begging for luck
or a Yankee buck.
Take heed,
Big Brother.
Life sucks
when you're down
on your luck,
flat
on your back.
Boxed up
like
a heap
of discarded
flat-pack.

Manhattan, NYC
March 14

The Penn

I caught the Huntington train from Penn Station at 10:35 a.m.
Red and blue leatherette seats
in a three-two combination.
Steel and Formica.
I'd seen nothing quite like her before.
We came out of the tunnel
into clear blue skies
and sunlight.

Train journey from NYC to Cold Spring Harbor, Long Island
March 15

Cold Spring Harbor, Long Island

Most of the afternoon
I spent trudging around
St. John's Cemetery
in Sleepy Hollow,
trying to locate Otto Kahn's grave.

What of Oheka Castle?
The house looked smaller than I had imagined from the outside
but larger inside.
The oaken silence of the library
chatters once more
with feet and inquisitive fingers.
That in itself cannot be a bad thing.

I met the owner Gary Melius
and his delightful daughter Nancy.
They both reside at the house.
Gary occupies Otto's suite.
Nancy treated me to lunch
and spent a good half-hour
escorting me around the house.
She then drove me to St. John's Church and Cemetery
to help me search for Otto's grave.
We didn't find it.

I returned to Manhattan by train,
physically exhausted
and still unable to find anywhere
that serves a decent pot of tea.
New York City is crying out
for a chain of traditional English cafés.

Cold Spring Harbor, Long Island
March 15

I returned to Manhattan by train

Where Have You Been?

'Where have you been?'
asked the waitress behind the bar.
'I've been reading away,' I said.
'You fancy a desert'?
My tum's a little too full
to push anything else inside.
Just chilling, letting it slide.
Sarah Vaughan has the right idea.
Keep the diners waiting.
St. Patrick's Day looms
on the other side of midnight.
Green leprechauns and all that.
Even the soy sauce bottle
in the restaurant
has a green top.
How strange is that!
Spooky, spooky.
Life in the key of green.
Music to chew spinach to.

Wagamama, Nomad/Flatiron (dinner)
210 Fifth Avenue (at 26th St.), NYC
March 16

The Flatiron Building, 175 Fifth Avenue, NYC

Bosie Tea Parlor

In my quest for a real pot of tea,
I finally found a café
that serves tea as it should taste.
The Bosie Tea Parlor in Greenwich Village
is as welcome as an oasis is
to a camel.
Now, which tea to choose
from the large variety on offer.
I narrowed it down to three: [4]

Organic Golden Monkey
Grown in the Fujian province, this black tea has a subtle richness and a
pleasant aftertaste. It goes beautifully with milk and sweetener or on its
own. Price per pot: $8 small, $14 large.

Ajiri
A strong and smooth tea, this CTC (crush, tear, curl) tea from Kenya has
won the popular vote for the best black tea at the 2012 and 2013 World
Tea Expo. Price per pot: $6 small, $10 large.

Nilmini FOP [5]
Grown along the southern border of the Sinharaja Rain Forest, this
smooth, full-bodied Ceylon cannot be found anywhere else in the States.
We are very proud to carry this Ahinsa from the Nilmini Estate, an organic
garden practicing the biodiversity model. Price per pot: $7 small, $12
large.

I opt for Organic Golden Monkey.

---

[4] All the tea descriptions are taken from *The Bosie Tea Parlor Tea Book* and are
reproduced courtesy of Bosie Tea Parlor.
[5] FOP – Flowery Orange Pekoe.

There was
one further tea
that attracted my attention,
Irish Breakfast,
as appropriately,
today is St. Patrick's Day.

Irish Breakfast
Our special Irish Breakfast blend is a detectably robust mix of premium
African and Indian teas. It is full-bodied without being overly astringent,
and quite a bit stronger than its English counterpart. Price per pot: $6
small, $10 large.

The bill came
inserted
on page 37
inside a copy
of *Here is New York*
by E.B. White.
I shall now have to purchase
a copy of the book.
This I did
at a bookstore [6]
around the corner
from the café
in the Village.

Bosie Tea Parlor, 10 Morton Street, West Village,
Greenwich Village, NYC (afternoon tea) [7]
March 17

---

[6] bookbook, 266 Bleecker Street, West Village, NYC.
[7] Bosie Tea Parlor is moving to new premises at 506 LaGuardia Place in June 2019.

The Moon's on Fire

The moon's on fire.
It'll be out in two more minutes.
The apple crumble, that is.
A spoon would be helpful.
A fork as well.
The elegance and mystique New York once had,
has now sadly faded.
Faceless modern high-rise buildings
block the view.
Their windows reflect the pain
we're all subjected to.
Trump Tower,
liar, liar,
the moons on fire.
'Ghost town'
plays on the stereo.
It's someone's birthday in this cold city,
but it's not mine.
Andy Warhol is now a parking lot.
Audrey Hepburn's the new girl
on the block.
What would he have thought?
And still, the Village people flock to the YMCA.
Bloomingdale's has sunk into retail oblivion,
and there's a big apple in Grand Central Terminal.
Praise Hallelujah for Jackie Kennedy,
for without her, where would the trains stop?

Massoni, 11 East 31 Street, NYC (dinner)
March 17

Main: Bell and Evans chicken breast, cacciatore, castle valley butcher polenta $28
Pudding: Homemade apple pie $7
Drink: San Pellegrino sparkling water $8

praise Hallelujah for Jackie Kennedy, . . .

for without her, where would the trains stop?

New York (II)

The wide expanse of the Hudson River
makes the notion of being on an island
a reality.
As E.B. White astutely perceived
in his short account, *Here is New York,*[8]
there are roughly three New Yorks:
First, the city known to those citizens born and bred in it;
Second, the metropolis trodden by commuters;
And finally, the one that entices an individual born elsewhere
in search of fulfilling an ambition or desire.
I wonder if I might add a fourth?
New York viewed through the eyes of a tourist,
an observer, on the sidelines of life.
A visitor, no sooner here than gone.
Resplendent in their ignorance.
Chasing nothing further than their nose.
Brief, composite, and fiercely unyielding
A buff representation of the city served on a salver
much like a hog roast.
Purely for the event.
My New York is undoubtedly that of the tourist.
How else am I to view it?

New York's heart
no longer beats
to the sound of the city;
it beats
in pursuit
of the dollar.

---

[8] White, E.B. *Here is New York,* publ. Harper & Brothers, 1949.

LE LABO INC. – Manufacturers of Fine Perfumery

New York (III)

I purposely did not see the annual St. Patrick's Day Parade today.
I did, however, see many revelers molesting the streets on their way to it.

Though I am a Celt,
I have no Irish ancestry
to talk bravely about.

My presence,
though welcome,
would have been akin
to gatecrashing a party
thrown by a stranger.

I felt no desire
to daub green war paint
and glitter
upon my skin.
And neither did I
wish to wear
a pint of Guinness
upon my head
in the guise
of a felt floppy hat.

The parade took place
as scheduled,
but I had no sight
nor sound of it
marching southwards
along Fifth Avenue;
such is the peculiar grid of streets
that mark Manhattan.

The parade came and went,
as did the green glitter
and string beads,
many of which were swiftly discarded
into trash cans.

life in the key of green - St. Patrick's Day muffins [9]

---

[9] Magnolia Bakery, Dining Concourse, Grand Central Terminal, 42nd Street at Park Avenue.

Canada

Amtrak (I)

Today I travel to Montreal
in a tin can on wheels
courtesy of Amtrak.

The Adirondack lakes
are partially frozen over
and look 'partially' awesome.

It's exactly 15:02 p.m.,
and the train
is slicing its way
through the rocky hillside.
The Adirondacks
and its lakes
have an earnest look of Mahler to them.
Snatches of sunlight
make little difference
upon the ice-covered lakes.
A March hare
Leaps.
Field after field of symmetrical vines
hibernating,
patiently waiting
for the caress of spring
to bring them back to life.
Forests of deciduous trees.
Their bare, grey, withered branches
reach out
in stark contrast.

"Get your papers ready for border control"
came the call.

At Plattsburgh, New York,
the train halts.
Belligerent smokers
leap off the train
onto the platform
to inhale nicotine.

Plattsburgh, NY

At the Canadian border
a field of mallards welcomes us.
The cornfield was wreathing
with birds.

Further into Canada,
fields of snow
on both sides of the rails
spread out before us.
And all the time,
the train blows its deep, hollow horn,
informing locals
of its imminent approach.

The late afternoon sun
bounces off the tracks
like whispers
in a vast empty hall.
And all the neatly kept wooden houses
yawn as we pass by.

The train is now half-empty,
having deposited travellers
not Montreal bound.
And still, the angry growl
from the driver's horn
continues to forewarn locals
of its approach.
A soundtrack
that has travelled with me
for nigh on ten hours.

Long shadows
across the flat, barren landscape.
Tufts of twigs
splash a touch
of interest.
Along the rail side,
steel telegraph pylons,
like 4-legged aliens,
seize your attention.
A thick layer of snow
carpets every square acre
far beyond the curve
of my eye.

On my left,
a whole field of pylons
appears from nowhere
and disappears just as fast.

A motorway
with little traffic

cozies up alongside
the track.

We arrive at *Gare Centrale*
in Montreal
early evening.

Amtrak train from Penn Station to Montreal
March 19

snatches of sunlight upon ice-covered lakes – the Adirondacks

Farine Five Roses

Hold that note.
A quarter past nine.
The piano player nods
as he plays the old upright
wedged into a corner
inside the Polish café bazaar
on Rue St Paul
in old town Montreal.

I bet you didn't know,
I can play the piano.

I asked the waiter,
Farine Five Roses,
does it really exist?
'I pass by it every day,'
he assured me,
with a glint in his smile.
Farine Five Roses.

Turn right outside
and then first left.
Head to the Port,
and you'll see it
Farine Five Roses
on the rooftop,
standing proud.
Red lettering
lighting up the sky.

Farine Five Roses,
'I pass by it every day.'

Starter: *Zupa dnia*: Soup of the day
Chicken and Barley and homemade rye bread C$6
Main: *Kotlet Z Drobiu*
Breaded chicken breast served with potatoes, salad of the day (homemade coleslaw without mayo) and Dijon sauce C$20
Pudding: Fruit (apple) cobbler served with sweet cream C$6

Stash Café (Polish restaurant) (dinner)
200 rue St-Paul Ouest, Montreal
March 21

Farine Five Roses   photograph by Carlos Viani (Montreal) [10]

---

[10] After viewing the striking Farine Five Roses hoarding, I returned to Le Petit Hotel, where I was staying. At the reception desk, I relayed my evening's events to the concierge and told him how a photograph I'd seen in a local magazine had inspired it all. He asked if I would read him the account I'd jotted down. This I did. When I finished reading it, he had a look of surprise on his face. It was then he told me his name was Carlos Viani, and the picture that had inspired me was his.

Amtrak (II)

Ice flows
like jigsaw pieces.
No two are the same.
A hovercraft effortlessly
glides along the river
towing a tug.
Farewell Montreal,
my time is done.
Back on the silver bullet train
travelling to New York Penn Station.
Outside,
snow, like frothy milk,
glistens in the morning sun
as if waiting to be sucked up
through a straw.
Shadows heightened.
Footprints lengthened,
imprinted haphazardly,
bringing a whole new perspective to the landscape.

Our first stop
Saint-Lambert arrives,
then the US border at midday.
I'll be back in the Big Apple
by nightfall
in the warmer environs
of the Sanctuary Hotel.

The train halts
at the American border.
Inside
we all wait
for border guards
to board.

The curve in the track
allows me a view of the train
and the three front coaches
berthed
alongside the railroad station.
Nothing fancy,
just a plain, brick building
with windows
and a door.
And three distinct wooden telegraph poles
with porcelain
and glass
electrical conductors
upon their arms,
like sparrows;
still, unmoving,
watching everything below.

The temperature drops.
I put on my heavy jacket
and peer out of the window,
watching snow melt.
Nobody saw that
except me.

This land they call America
is grand beyond belief,
in scale, and in imaginings,
laid out beneath my feet.
This land they call aplenty
is all those things and more.
Where nothing goes to futile waste,
with opportunity galore.

Plattsburgh, NY

The lake reaches out
as far as the horizon,

whence snow-capped mountains
rise and touch the sky.
Red rocks
lay strewn aside the tracks.
Remnants of the engineers
that constructed the railway
over one hundred years ago.
The train cuts through the hillside
like a warm knife through butter.
Should anything go amiss
on the tight hazardous bends,
it's a sheer drop to the lake below,
where sit wooden chalets
sprinkled upon the shoreline.
Vacation homes
for the well-heeled.
The sun is out to play.

Fort Edward, NY
Saratoga Springs, NY
Schenectady, NY
Albany-Rensselaer, NY
Hudson, NY
Rhinecliff-Kingston, NY
Poughkeepsie, NY
Croton-Harmon, NY
Yonkers, NY

There are too many maggots
in the Big Apple
to make a good apple pie.

What you know
is not always
what you want to know.

three distinct telegraph poles, Rouses Point [11]

America (II)

March

Syracuse

In Syracuse, during the last week in August
and the first week in September,
the townsfolk hold a big country fair.
Syracuse is where my mother was born.

---

[11] Sketch by I.C. Williams.

The Ballet Dancer

A young girl
dressed head to foot
in white
dances ballet
solo
around the statue
in Columbus Circle.
I watch
from a balcony
overlooking.

Columbus Circle, NYC
March 23

Kooky

So, this is New York City.
How lucky am I?
Some things
are not obvious
to the human eye.
Dinner at the Algonquin.
Where the oak wood
still
looks black,
and Dorothy Parker
still holds court
peering down
from an oil painting
hanging
on the restaurant lobby wall.
Who could forget Matilda,
the hotel's feline,
now replaced by Hamlet,
Shakespeare's cat?
The penguins
are mightily odd
around here.
A little bit dropsy
like the cascading chandeliers.
Truth be told,
bristly and cold,
unlike the ambience
which never grows old.

A match
for a matchless hero.
The Algonquin
beats
the lot.

From 1920s fiction
to a screenplay
with an everyday plot.
Harpo Marx
and the ghost of Woollcott
still appear
in the shadows
between
floors,
in the elevator,
and behind doors.
Justin Timberlake territory
it is not.
Truth be told,
I kinda like it kooky.
Kooky and old.

The Algonquin Hotel (dinner)
59 West 44th Street, NYC
March 23

America

Of this vast land,
I know little
that would enrich
a geographical text.
Nor could I adlib
expressively
of its contour lines
at some public address.
Though, in my mind,
my thoughts are clear.
This land of hope and plenitude
is no island
unreachable by man,
untouched by
human hands.
This land is ploughed
and tamed of bough.
A nation
in which its people
live and sweat their brow.
With ne'er a reason
to be lame.
This is a land
of mighty things.
Of swallows and starling
and hummingbird wings.
This is a land that sings.

The Algonquin Hotel (dinner)
59 West 44th Street, NYC
March 23

On March 24, I caught the Green Train number 5 from Grand Central Terminal to Eastern Parkway, Brooklyn, where I visited Brooklyn Museum to see *David Bowie IS.*

New York (IV)

New York.
The 7 digits of greed
pointiing straiight at you.
This is Wall Street.
Grab a $ here.
Good morniing passengers.
Do not hold the doors.
Transfer is availlable.
Insert your credit card.
No use
trying to hide
your face.
We captured you on CCTV.
God looks down
on the human race.

David Bowie is
in town.
Brooklyn Museum
wears his crown.
Meet and greet
with an old acquaintance.
You and Rudi
down Wardour Street.
Strung out in Soho.
Love is a turnaround.
Nothing much going on,
just publicity.
We made our own
amusement.

The queues are out
to ogle,
stare,
and poke fun
at his orange hair.
But would those very same people
have stood beside him
back on Wardour Street
in old Blighty
all those years ago!
Guess not.
Too surreal
for the bourgeoisie.

Memories multiply
at times like these.
Heightened by the
hypocrisy
of gentlefolk,
blinded by tradition,
playing life by rules
and conditions.

So what did I think?
A divine mess.
The missing third hand.
Pubic hair.
Kenny's Chelsea pad.
'A man Dali.'

Ironically
Bowie found his high
and reclaimed his life
when he quit drugs.
That's the one positive
I took away
with me,
that

and the
Brooklyn Bridge.

Green Train number 5 to Brooklyn Museum
March 24

David Bowie Is at Brooklyn Museum

Blue

Blue to me
is not
what blue is
to you.
Magnificent,
Ageless,
with the honour of ancient Pharaohs.

I'm open to suggestions
should the need arise
but not
when it offends
my liberty
or leads
to compromise.
The colour
arranges,
protects,
and wages.
Blue
is my empathy,
not enmity.

Brooklyn Museum
Brooklyn, NY
March 24

The Wisest Owl I Ever Did Meet

Brooklyn Museum owl

The wisest owl I ever did meet
was perched upon a windowsill,
and in his sight, a mouse did see
his dinner on a platter.

As still, as still, as still could be.
He watched the mouse intensely.
And when the time to pounce arrived,
he swooped an *arc de Triomphe*.

And in his mouth,
the mouse's tail
did wriggle, and wiggle,
squirm and worm,
and slap its way around
the owl's jaw.

Until the owl's throat did burn
with pain.
Enough to make the owl hoot.
And as he did,
the mouse fell out.

And tumbled through the air
at speed
until the mouse
did fall to earth.
And as it landed
with a thump upon its head,
the mouse was heard
to say out loud,
'Am I still here or am I dead?'

To which the wisest owl I ever met
was heard to shriek,
'I like a mouse that's off its head,'
and swooped again
and slurped it up.

In one foul gulp,
the mouse was gone,
no longer on this planet earth.

Deep down inside the owl's stomach,
the mouse wriggled,
and wiggled,
squirmed and wormed,

and how it turned
the owl's head in wonderment.

And then it said,
"Are you still here, or are you dead?"
To which the mouse
was heard to squeak,
"I'm dead."

Brooklyn Museum
Brooklyn, NY
March 24

view towards Manhattan from Brooklyn Bridge

crossing Brooklyn Bridge

Rockefeller Plaza

Rows of flags
blowing in the breeze
like garments
on a washing line.
Limp
yet magnificent.
Iridescent
in colour,
some more so
than others.
Red dominates,
then white
and blue.
Rockefeller Plaza
is but
a restless hew,
complicated
by the presence
of a thousand eyes
rising
up
towards the sky
as the world
looks down
upon Rockefeller Plaza.

Rockefeller Plaza, NYC
March 25

a thousand eyes rising up towards the sky

Rockefeller Plaza

The Observationalist (I)

If I head out to sea
on a voyage of discovery,
would you miss me?
Of all the ways to go
It seems the most pleasant,
If you could call it so.

Wind turbines frolicking on the horizon.
Voices carried on the wind.
A dog's bark echoes.

At times like this,
I always think of treasure
lost long ago,
washed up on the shore.
But what I find,
is not what I expect.
Fresh worm mounds,
seawater puddles,
very few shells.
Occasional clumps of seaweed.
Mysterious footprints.
Footprints!

And the sea continues retreating,
keeping its secrets
for another day,
not today.

A hippopotamus face.
The shape of a frog.
Rock formations.
A rotting groyne
covered in spiral and toothed wrack.

I watch my steps
as I navigate a clear path.
The observationalist
in me
returns,
as the hungry sea
creeps silently back
to the shore.

Worthing
March 31

seawater puddles - Worthing beach

The Observationalist (II) Movements

I can't ever remember waking up
and looking out directly at the sea.
Its water flushed
halfway towards the penciled brow
of the horizon.
7:49 a.m.,
Easter Monday,
with hardly a soul about
except
a dog walker
in the distance
playing catch ball
with a hound.
I stand motionless
at the third-floor window,
observing.
The occasional vehicle drives by,
trailed by a solitary jogger
hugging the path.
Drizzle dancing upon shallow puddles
gives movement to the road.
A pair of shifty-looking seagulls
tap-dance on a grassy mound,
enticing earthworms up.
The annelids have no chance,
even at this early time of the morning.
If the weather
was a little more clement,
I might be inclined
to go for a run.
A warm shower beckons.
Miserable days
don't stop the world
from going about its business.

Things to do.
A visitor,
perhaps!
My book to review.
A trip to arrange.
Movements
on my horizon
to contemplate.

Worthing
April 2

The Observationalist (III)

Waves,
like moving steps,
guide my vision
ahead,
across a vastness,
as wide
as it is deep,
as the sky
itself.

The promise
of a free meal
brings the gulls
lapping
at the water's edge,
where sand
now reveals
its complexion;
perfectly natural,
bathed in the moisture
of a million tears.

There is no louder sound
than that of the wind
howling inside your head.
That, and the crashing
of waves
battering pebbles
violently against rocks
in a rage.

Where hope stops,
prayer begins.
A melodrama played out
at sea.

A sailor's grave
is where we bathe.
How forgetful we
humans can be.
We
and the hungry sea.

Worthing
April 2

The Gift

What would I ask of you
if I had the right to do so?
I would be spoilt for choice.
Of that, I can be truthful.
'Tis not for me to question,
nor churlishly dismiss,
the gift of love you offer
is more priceless than a wish.

Worthing
April 2

The Soldier [12]

This noble isle
speaks loud and just
of trials of past
and future.
Imperium
inscribed in dust
of loyal soldiers
bearing scars
from war and sabre.
Held in the name
of Majesty
and Common Law.
Be standing
in thine honour.
I place laurels
upon your brow
in gratitude and awe
for your servitude
and toils.
Your names are ne'er forgotten.
Each and every life.
Such selflessness.
My deference,
I lay before your feet.

Brighton
April 3

---

[12] In remembrance of my grand-uncle Pvt. John Balmain Williams, Royal Scots, b. 1877 – d. 25 April 1918.

Kiss Me First

Kiss me first.
I ask only that of you.
For when the space
between us
grows,
the memory of that kiss
will fill
the void
with treasure
and bring us back
together.

Brighton
April 3

The Hotel Grand

The Grand
is not so grand
these days.
Its past lives
more in memory
than in name
are painted on plaster
from several decades ago.
When crinolines
swept the stairs,
and priceless jewels
glistened brighter
than the chandeliers
suspended in the lobby.

Beneath the bronze statue
of a crouching boy
with arms outstretched
and head bowed,
where the gentry
once gathered
sipping cocktails,
the cocktails still chatter
but to a different tune.
New money
for old booze.
The penance of which
is more to amuse.

Each night
the *maître d'hôtel*
performs
his balancing act,
much like a circus ringmaster
working the room.

He is but a caricature
conjuring attention.
And did I mention
the slow-walking waitress,
more haughty
than naughty,
earning her tips
from the sway
of her hips?

Lest I forget,
the long-legged waiter
who straddles
plastered columns
with pointed feet.
More Cleese
than cleavage.
As lean
as a runner bean.
'Your usual, Sir?'
The mark of experience
of a waiter
that never forgets.

On this very night
forty-four years ago
in this same city,
Abba won Eurovision
and, by coincidence,
were staying
in this very hotel.
The winners truly took it all.

The Hotel Grand, Brighton
April 6

the winding staircase at the Hotel Grand, Brighton

The Little Boy Full of Joy

The little boy full of joy
is happier than you or me.
For the little boy
of playful joy
can see beyond
the gloomy sky,
where doubts and fears
and uncertainty dwell.
He has no sight
of Dante's Hell.
For the little boy
of boundless joy
can see
what we cannot.
The little boy
of blissful joy
can do
what we cannot.

Of scary monsters,
he has no fear.
Of clouded forecasts,
his sight is clear.
No misery or pain
can sour
his playful games.
His vision is beyond
that which mere mortals attain.
For the little boy
of endless joy
is blessed with sight
far greater
than you
dare ever guess.

For the little boy
of immeasurable joy,
though blind,
is blessed
with an inner eye
as clear and pure
as the crystal tears
Niobe rock
doth weep.

If I could perform miracles,
I would give them all to him.
Yet, I doubt
the miracles I give
would be of use
to him.
For never
in my life
have I seen
a happier boy
than the little boy
full of joy
I saw playing
in the Hotel Grand.

The Hotel Grand, Brighton
April 6

Suburbia Land

Nothing much happens in suburbia.
Another night in transience,
much like any other.
A cat on the wall,
a dog, and a bark.
Good neighbors
tucked up indoors
in their plush sofa chairs,
little going on.

Nothing much happens
behind their front door.
Even less on TV,
in suburbia land.
No wonder there's a
drug and alcohol issue.
Who needs life
when you can get off your head
for the price of a pint
and the roll of a dice.

Give me a good horror movie,
and I'll be satisfied.
Give me recognition,
not ammunition.
A bullet in the throat
is no good for my voice.
What I need is hope,
not a bloodstained shirt.

The kids don't work,
and your dad's a jerk.
What's the use of monogamy
when no one listens to me.

Misery and injury,
self-inflicted *ange doux,*
just for you.
Don't you hate the zoo
almost as much as I hate you?
Another night in suburbia land.
Nothing much happens in suburbia.

Worthing
April 9

Superbowl Twister, Worthing promenade

The Lobster Ran off With The Lamb

Waiter: 'The only thing not on the menu
 is the lobster and the lamb.'

Iain: 'So, the lobster ran off with the lamb!'

 'Kind of. We're now waiting to see what
 the kids turn out like.'

 'In that case, I'll have the skate.'

 'With the *beurre blanc* and caper sauce?'

 'You bet, and mashed potatoes and
 mushy peas.'

 'Good choice.'

 A few moments later, I overheard a lady
 dining with two friends at the table next
 to me say, 'We'll split the bill in three.'

1st Friend: 'I don't think that's possible.'

2nd Friend: 'Good choice.'

The Fish Factory, Worthing
April 10

Where Once

Where once a fireplace stood,
there now is none.
The brick face welcomes you
with a frown.
Big changes are on the horizon.
Maybe a visit to India
or a trip to the Himalayas.
I've been to America
on a plane.
At times it felt like home
while at other times,
I felt alone.
Hot Chocolate on the sound system,
'So You Win Again,'
reminding me of Mickie,
Dave, Barbara, and Granville.
Dancing backward
to *Top of the Pops.*
Bring back the Seventies.
What was it all for?
If nothing,
then nothing at all.
I think I've found my elixir,
fish, and pudding.
Perhaps open a tree restaurant,
selling only that.
Be novel.
I swear I get tipsy
drinking non-alcoholic.

Crabshack, Worthing
April 13

Upon that Journey

Wipe the tear
from your face.
Act as if I never existed.
Scathe my toes
with bramble bushes.
Break my nose
with stones.
Build no alter in my name.
Lay no flowers
upon my grave.
Omit my name
from registers.
Pretend I never happened.
I have little else to give,
and what I have
is of no use
to either soul or heart,
for I have wished
my last request,
may God my witness
from him be blessed.
If nothing else,
I hope my time
among the fields
of rape and corn
have stood to prove
in countenance
did find
that man alone
did walk this earth,
and upon that journey
was laid to rest.

Worthing
April 14

man alone did walk this earth - Upon that Journey

Writings

Nothing will change.
Absolutely nothing.
Would that it could.
I've been that good.
Given up all my vices.
Not once but twice.
Offered up as penance
everything I owned.
If summer was wine,
I'm in the bowels of winter.
I spoke to God
inside Chichester Cathedral.
He listened.
The choir was singing
while my soul was talking.
I prayed for guidance.
He listened.
Thirteen pence in my pocket.
I offered you gold.
You gave me frankincense.

Outside, the rain hobbled.
Footsteps echoed
along the cobbles,
where horse-drawn carriages
once passed,
dropping lovers
into the cusp of night.
I found a place to shelter.
Christ looked down
from the street lantern.
His face as clear
as I was near.
Nothing has changed.
Absolutely nothing.

I'm not afraid;
of that, I am sure.
For when I'm gone,
the bells will chime
thirteen times.
Once for every penny,
I placed in your coffers.

Chichester Cathedral, Chichester
April 16

Christ looked down from the street lantern - Chichester

Eat Here

"Eat Here," says the sign.
"Homemade"
The tin plaque in question
is a curved arrow
and would have hung
above
or
beside an entrance.
Pre-war (WWII),
by the looks of it.
White background.
Enameled.
Chipped and rusty in parts,
with blue lettering
in capitals.

The metal sign
now leans upright
in a window
against the wall
with the arrow
pointing
outside
through the window
into the street.

It might once
have been illuminated,
perhaps with fluorescent light.
Now it rests forlornly
but comfortably
gathering dust.
Gone is the gaiety,
appealing lust

that attracted many
hungry guts.
"Eat Here" –
tasty homemade food
waiting to be consumed.
Heel my scars.
Lick my wounds.
How many eyes
did it once attract?
How many succumbed
to its enticing appeal?
'Eat Here'
'Eat Here'

And then it was gone.
The diners disappeared.
Only the sign remains
to remind you
that people ate here.

Worthing
April 17

The Artist & The Writer

The role of an artist
is to make life look
impossibly beautiful
or to tell the truth,
one or the other.
There is no in-between.
The role of the writer
is to colour those bits in-between.

Worthing
April 17

Jogging in a Wedding Dress

Jogging in a wedding dress
along the promenade.
Double looks
from passersby,
and not a groom in sight.
The sea is out forever,
never to return.
I bet the fish are angry
at losing their big home.

Worthing Seafront
April 19

Lottery

If I could win the lottery
and have money to burn,
I'd build a writer's library
and fill it up with words.
I'd call it The Williams
and plant a cornerstone,
upon which I'd inscribe,
Laid by an unknown.

Worthing
April 19

Poem

A knock to my bonce,
not twice but once.
Boy, did it hurt
and bloodied my shirt.

Worthing
April 19

I Have a Brother

I have a brother,
Andrew is his name.
He used to live next door to me.
I'd see him in his bedroom window,
peering down into our yard.
We never shared a single word,
just looked across at one another.

Year after year
I watched him grow
into a handsome young boy,
The brother that I never knew.
I owe him this,
if not a kiss,
a mention in my book.
The brother that I never had,
the brother that I wished.

Crabtree Lane
was where we lived
next door to one another.
Crabtree Lane
was where we lived
apart for many years.
How strange
now I look back
that this should be.
Questions, unanswered,
left abandoned
in the garden
that's grown in between.

Worthing
April 19

Seat M14

Thank you for sitting next to me
in seat M14.
I could see you
from the corner of my eye.
The cinema was largely empty,
maybe twenty at the most,
and out of every person seated,
you chose me
to sit next to a ghost.

You stayed and watched the entire film
right up until the credits.
*The Guernsey Literary
& Potato Peel Pie Society,*
just staring ahead
at the screen.

I kept watch
from the corner of my eye,
and when a tear rolled
down my cheek,
you never flinched.
You stayed beside me
until the end.
Then,
as I stood up to leave,
the lights came on,
and as I turned
to look at you,
the seat was empty.
Your spirit was gone.

Dome Cinema, Worthing
April 20

you chose me to sit next to - Dome Cinema, Worthing, at dusk

The Man With a Permanent Smile on His Face

Light grey, almost white hair.
Clean-shaven.
High forehead.
Rosy complexion,
with large rubbery ears.
A half-a-saucer mouth,
narrow eyes,
and an ample, rectangular nose.
He could almost pass for a Scandinavian.
An outdoor type,
a keen hill walker.
Aged late fifties.
Well preserved.
Healthy looking.
The man with a permanent smile on his face.

Chichester
May 1

Princess Patience Blues

Notting Hill
has lost its thrill.
Its guts
have been ripped out.
Replaced
with fake designer ones
and even faker
goods.
The price
of a community
is now measured by
a label.
Bring back the squats
where lovers lived,
not the fake tanned
arse wipes
who sup trendy Gin
and wash their skin
in horse manure.
Princess Patience Blues
is written on my shoes,
with every step I take
along Westbourne Grove
and Portobello Road.
Princess Patience Blues
imprinted on my soul.
Oh, Notting Hill,
what have they done
to one
so beautiful
as you?

Notting Hill Gate, London
May 13

The Glass Noodle House

In the glass noodle house,
you tempted me,
injected my pain,
corrected me.

In the chocolate apothecary
where fishtails once laid,
I took tea, ate a cookie,
and watched yachts sail.
I then took bus number 4
to Queen Victoria's front door.
I bet you didn't know
I could do things alone.
Returned to the mainland
on a catamaran
from the Island of Wight,
none of which I planned.

Isle of Wight
May 20

returned to the mainland on a catamaran - Ryde Harbor, Isle of Wight

Secret

If I loaned you a secret,
would you know
how to keep it
safe
under lock and key
in your memory?
And if I asked
for it back,
would you willingly
return it,
or would you simply reply,
"What secret! You never gave me one."

Train journey from Chichester to London
May 27

Jazz Hands

"Bang on,"
I heard you say.
"Bang on,"
as you strut my way.
Hands gesticullating
which way forth.
Stance of a wide boy.
Hoodie like a monk.
Your mouth a weapon
with which you melodize.
"Bang on,"
a flick of the wrist.
A muscle spasm.
Fingers splayed.
A coded message to the rich.
"Fuck you,"
my columbine.
Your word is your *raison d'être,*
and I'm no liar.

Worthing
May 31

92

The Three Maharajas, Worthing

take a **leaf** …

out of my **book**
attach it to a **branch**
watch it **grow**

leaf … **book** … **branch** … **grow**

Printed in Great Britain
by Amazon